BEGINNERS GUIDE 2 GENEALOGY

THE 6 STEPS TO START

YOUR FAMILY TREE

by Danielle Brackenbury

ISBN: 9798563571501

Contents

Every ancestry path is different	4
What do you actually know?	6
Do I have Proof?	9
Genealogical Proof Standard	10
Explanation of Record Types	11
Offline Software Vs. Online Subscriptions	14
Interview Older Relatives	18
Do any old photographs exist	22
Have any books been written about any of your family branches	26
Where do your ancestors live?	27
What genealogy resources are available in your area?	29
Free Charts and Templates	30
Record Resources	31
Software	37
About the Author	39

Every ancestry path is different so let's find out where yours takes you. I know you are as excited as I am to get started so let's jump right in!

Genealogy can be a challenge. If you are just starting you may be asking yourself where do I begin. Here are 6 Steps to Start Your Family Tree in order to get off to a good start on your ancestry journey.

Genealogy can be a fun and rewarding hobby. Knowing where you come from and being able to hand that knowledge down to future generations can be very rewarding and can make you feel very good. Most of us have heard family stories about our ancestors. Some are funny or amazing but most turn out to be just that, funny or amazing stories.

The good news is that the reality of what your ancestors went through can be far more interesting than fiction. Most genealogists want to research all the time. Many people do not realize that genealogy is something anyone can do.

As with any new endeavor there are some basic things that you should know that way you know the best place to start. These are the Six questions you need to ask yourself before you start researching your family tree.

What do you actually know?

As researchers we have all asked ourselves the same question at one point or another, where do I start? We will start at the beginning and build step by step. Genealogy can be very over-whelming so do not let that turn into discouragement.

Start by identifying what you do know. You might just be surprised at what you already can piece together from your own life experiences. Write down what you already know. Don't focus on what you don't. Focus first on the hard facts and leave family stories as just that, stories until proven accurate.

Never be afraid to reach out in the blogs and research question threads on the websites we go over. Distant cousins who have been researching before can be wonderful resources for your re-search. Just keep searching. Being able to organize and document what you find is key...

There are some examples of Charts and Records Sheets below to help keep you organized. You can find free resources for blank copies of these sheets in our resources section below. In this step it will give you the tools to be efficient and organized which will allow you to gauge your progress.

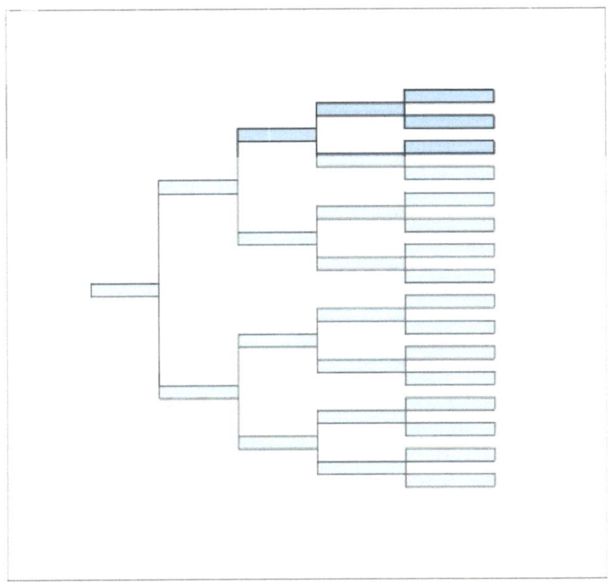

There are some examples of Charts and Records Sheets below to help keep you organized. You can find free resources for blank copies of these sheets in our resources section below. In this step it will give you the tools to be efficient and organized which will allow you to gauge your progress.

Mythology is not Genealogy!

A proof statement can be defined as being a set of supporting documentations that prove to be true. When new evidence arises any proof statement may need reevaluation.

Genealogical Proof Standard

(GPS) Ethics and Standards are the best practices to enable researchers to come as close as possible to what actually happened in the past.

In order to reach a sound conclusion we need to try to meet all five components.

- Research has been conducted with reasonably exhaustive measures.

- Each fact has a complete source citation so you and other researchers know where you found it.

- The evidence is reliable and has been properly interpreted.

- All contradictions have been solved.

- The conclusion has been soundly reasoned and logically written down.

Even if you have known something about your family your whole life, do you have any proof in the form of vital records, court documents, military records, old newspaper records, or other things to back it up?

In Genealogy, everything should be questioned, so you must have proof of something before you put it on your family tree.

Explanation of Record Types

This is in no way an extensive list of the types of documents available to researchers.

- **Land grants** -

A land grant is a grant of public land, to any institution, organization, or to particular groups of people.

- **Wills/Probates** -

The official proving of a will

- **U.S. Population Census** –

Population count every decade, demographics such as age, marital status, race, location, profession, land value, place of birth. These items are not included every time they take a census; different one is in different years. * Almost all of the 1890 census' population schedules were irreparably damaged by a fire in the Commerce Department Building in January of 1921. Remember that the census search uses the Soundex search. The Census takers would spell the names phonetically so variations of the same name are common.

- **Birth/Death Records** –

In 1630 laws were passed requiring the local church to keep the births and death records in the United States. Local towns, counties, and states started keeping census data for land and tax purposes. Then in 1840, the Census Bureau was created. A standard death certificate was not created until 1910.

- **Military Records**

Revolutionary War, War of 1812, War for Texas Independence, Spanish-American war, Marriage records, Voters Registration

ONLINE
OFFLINE

Offline Software vs Online Subscriptions

Make sure you match your skill level in your choice of software on genealogy and computer use that way it is functional for your needs. It is very important to have a place to document your findings so your work and effort will never be lost and can be passed down to future generations of your family. Remember that right now, you are just gathering data so don't rack your brain on proving it correct. Always document where you found the information to help with later evaluation.

Online monthly subscriptions can get pricey. After 15 years of researching I learned this the hard way! Hiring a professional genealogist can cost you thousands! What? I let you in on what I've learned. Family history doesn't have to be expensive, in fact many resources and products are available to you completely free.

Ancestral Quest Basic® connects two websites **RootsWeb**® and **Ancestry**®. This has a simple and easy design with an intuitive interface and as a bonus it automatically searches genealogical sites saving you time and effort.

My Heritage Family Tree Builder® is a free program which allows you to document and build your tree online and has digitized documents you can search. Unlimited information, create and print maps, import /export GEDCOM file

GRAMPS® **Genealogical Research and Analysis Management Program Systems**® gives you everything you need on a tech savvy level by having a simple interface, privacy option, and unicode support.

Legacy Family Tree® does have a free version of their program. It has simple easy design backed by powerful software. The free version contains most of the features of the paid version including unlimited data and people. If you have a GEDCOM file you can import it with this software.

Personal Ancestry Writer II® This is for all the Macintosh users. It isn't a high performing program but it is free. It has a simple design and will make your research easier to organize. You can clearly see the tools available. It is a good program for beginner Mac users.

Roots Magic Essentials® is a great beginner free genealogy software program. It is clear and understandable with easy navigation. Unlimited facts and people storage with tons of charts, unicode support and free upload or download of your GEDCOM file.

No matter which one of these completely free options you use to store your research you can rest assured it is safe and in good hands.

Interview Older Relatives

Interviewing older members of your family is an important part of getting started with your family history search. Who are the oldest people in your family? Are they willing to answer questions and share their stories? Some relatives in the older generations might be hesitant to talk about past events. This is how their generation was raised.

You can put their mind at ease by telling them that they will have a chance to see and approve of anything that you write before you share it with others. Your relatives that are in your life, cousins, aunts, uncles, and grandparents whoever that may be can be a wonderful resource and starting point. Words of caution remember to use your GPS (Genealogical Proof Standard) to guide you with family stories.

Consider them entertaining fiction until you find documentation to support the story. Family stories can get changed and embellished over the course of many years. I, myself, have proven just as many stories false as I have found to be true.

Be sure to take a notebook or journal when you talk to your

relatives. That way you can compare your list of questions and compare their stories with the facts. Start with an open ended question or topic you know will elicit a reply for example a story you have heard them tell in the past.

If the relative agrees, setting up a recorder in the room may help you to remember details. Sitting around the dinner table is a great way to get family stories flowing. Ask questions which encourage more than a yes or no answer. The best stories are full of feelings, facts, and descriptions.

Be a creative listener by showing interest and taking an active part in the dialogue. Try to keep your interview a reasonable amount of time so you do not wear each other out. I would suggest no longer than 2 hours. It's tiring for both of you and this is supposed to be fun for both of you. Consider preparing a transcript or written report as a tangible thank you to your relative for their cooperation.

If they get uncomfortable talking about just move on. Stay flexible; use your questions as a guideline only. They may have something they want to say to you that you never thought to ask. Don't interrupt or attempt to correct them as this can end an interview in a hurry. When you are done be sure to thank them for participating!

Do any old photographs exist?

Ask around to see who has the oldest photos in your family. Hopefully, they will allow you to view them or possibly make a copy to add to your research. Look in old boxes, trucks, and attics for any old photos or records you may have and not even realize. Be sure to post your research names into your profile on the websites you use to search. Distant cousins may reach out with details, artifacts, or photos.

Have you ever considered what other options beyond vital records are out there? You are only limited by your imagination. Other genealogical artifacts can be helpful as well. They can provide insights into an ancestor's life you will not find anywhere else. Items such as Newspapers, old diaries, and family bibles are wonderful resources.

Old Newspaper Articles and announcements may surprise you with many details in your ancestor's hometown newspaper that you never knew. Not every newspaper is digitized yet so reach out the local librarian in your ancestor's town. Most libraries have a genealogy section and many have on site researchers to look up articles for you.

Diaries have been kept for centuries. Although you may not find any hard facts or data, what you may find may be just as valuable. A unique first hand insight into your ancestor's day to day life. Learning who they were as people in their own authentic words is irreplaceable. A diary is a true family treasure.

Family Bibles are treasure troves of family information. It records births, deaths, and marriages in the family, sometimes going back generations. Bibles were most commonly kept in the

1700s and 1800s. These types of family records may contain information before vital records were ordered. You may also find people that were missed by the census records.

Photos, clothing, old furniture, handmade items and jewelry are things we normally think of as genealogical artifacts they are more accurately described as heirlooms. These types of items hold sentimental value but not many facts. Photos are the only exceptions to this as they can be both sentimental and informationally valuable.

Have any books been written about any of your family branches?

This will take some research to find out. If so, you should read them and you can use the information in the books in your own research as long as it is documented in the book and you properly cite the source in your research.

Many books have been digitized in online resources like Google Books for example but there are many more.

Where did your ancestors live?

Make a list of locations that you know. You will need this list if you ever visit local archives, cemeteries, and old homesteads of your ancestors. There is a very long list of places to research archives such as the public or county library in the location you are searching. This is in no way an exhaustive list.

If you are not sure, reach out to ask a question to the local librarian or local historical society in the location you want to research. Historical Societies and county courthouses are great places for resources. Most of these places have websites with archives and searchable databases. With the blessing of technology these records are becoming more and more digitized.

Hint * If you get stuck, Beginners Guide 2 Genealogy is always available to do research.

Feel free to reach out at our website

beginnersguide2genealogy.com

What genealogy resources
are available in your area?

Most areas have local genealogy libraries, archives, or historical societies. If your family has a history in the area, you will definitely want to visit them to see what information they have on your ancestors.

There is a very long list of places to research archives such as the public or county library in the location you are searching. This is in no way an exhaustive list. If you are not sure, reach out to ask a question to the local librarian or local historical society in the location you want to research.

Historical Societies and county courthouses are great places for resources. Most of these places have websites with archives and searchable databases. With the blessing of technology these records are becoming more and more digitized.

Free Charts and Templates

Charts are an efficient way to stay organized so you can review the details later after you find them in order to draw your conclusions.

National Genealogical Society

https://www.ngsgenealogy.org/free-resources/charts/

Vertex42

https://www.vertex42.com/ExcelTemplates/

family-tree-template.html

Record Resources

Us Census Bureau -

https://www.census.gov/

The US Census was taken National from 1850 to 2020. Legally they have released 1850 to 1940 to researchers. The US has privacy laws in place called the 72-year rule. It states that they will not release any information until 72 years after they collected it.

So, in 2022 the public will be able to view the 1950 census for the first time!!!! Not all of the following information is available in every census. Before the 1850 Census, few of these details were recorded. From 1790 to 1840, only the head of household is listed by name; other household members are merely counted in selected age groups.

Hint * Start with the 1940 census in your search and work your way backward.

Some information that the census records can include are: your ancestor's name, age at a certain point in time, state or country of birth, parents' birthplace(s), year of immigration, street address, marriage status and years of marriage, occupation, value of home and personal belongings.

National Archives Records Association - https://www.archives.gov/

The National Archives hold many records of great interest to genealogists. Here is a list of a few types of records you can find at the National Archives according to their own website. Census Records (1790-1940), Court Records, Immigration Records, Income Tax, Records of the Civil War Years.

Also, Land Records, Maps of interest to Genealogists, Maritime, Military Records, Native American Records, Naturalization Records, Naval Records, Passenger Lists, Passport Applications , Social Security Records, and Tax Records

Library of Congress -
https://loc.gov/

The Library of Congress has one of the world's premier collections of U.S. and foreign genealogical and local historical publications. The Library's genealogy collection began as early as 1815 with the purchase of Thomas Jefferson's library. The Library of Congress is in three buildings on Capitol Hill in Washington, D.C. It is the research library of the U.S. Congress. It is considered the national library of the United States. It's also the largest library in the world, with a collection of more than 170 million items.

US Genweb Project -

https://www.usgenweb.org/

The USGenWeb Project is a group of volunteers working together and having fun providing free online genealogy help and information for every Our national site provides links to state sites, which, in turn, provide gateways to the counties.

Freedmen's Bureau - http://www.freedmensbureau.com/

The Bureau of Refugees, Freedmen, and Abandoned Lands often referred to as the Freedmen's Bureau, was established in the War Department by an act of March 3, 1865. The Bureau supervised all relief and educational activities relating to refugees and freedmen, including issuing rations, clothing and medicine.

The Bureau also assumed custody of confiscated lands or property in the former Confederate States, border states, District of Columbia, and Indian Territory

JewishGen -

https://www.jewishgen.org/

The Global home for Jewish Genealogy. JewishGen serves as the global home for Jewish genealogy. Featuring unparalleled access to 30+ million records, it offers unique search tools, along with opportunities for researchers to connect with others who share similar interests.

Find A Grave -

https://www.findagrave.com/

Find the graves of ancestors, create virtual memorials or add photos, virtual flowers and a note to a loved one's memorial. Search or browse cemeteries and grave records for every-day and famous people from around the world.

Roots web -

https://home.rootsweb.com/

The Internet's oldest and largest free community.

Software

Ancestral quest basic - http://www.ancquest.com/AQBasics.htm

My Heritage Family Tree Builder - https://www.myheritage.com/family-tree-builder

GRAMPS

https://www.gramps-project.org/wiki/index.php?title=Download

Legacy Tree

https://legacyfamilytree.com/DownloadLegacy.asp

Personal Ancestry Writer PAWriter

http://lanopalera.org/Genealogy/AboutPAWriter.html

Roots Magic Essentials

http://www.rootsmagic.com/Essentials/

ABOUT THE AUTHOR

I have been a Family Researcher and Author. I have been researching for over 15 years in all parts of the United States. I enjoy helping people get started on their own journey of discovery so I have written a book and designed this course to help you get started without investing a fortune on professional researchers, documents, or membership fees. Let me share my knowledge with you so you can build an amazing detailed family tree. I have many techniques to share to build your Tree building skills and help you get started right away!! I have enjoyed working with my clients in the past and I look forward to teaching you how to start your Family Tree.

Contact Beginner's Guide 2 Genealogy
Website : http://www.beginnersguide2genealogy.com
Email dhobbstx@gmail.com
Facebook,Instagram,Google